To: Laura
with love
from: Dad and Mother 67"

D1302175

The Gift of Wonder

The Gift of Wonder

HELEN LOWRIE MARSHALL

Doubleday & Company, Inc. Garden City, New York

1967

To Stan

Whose steadfast belief
picks me up
and drives me to work

Library of Congress Catalog Card Number 67–28483
Copyright © 1967 by Helen Lowrie Marshall
All Rights Reserved
Printed in the United States of America

Contents

The Gift of Wonder

As daily now man conquers time and space,
And ways of stars and moon grow commonplace,
Dear God, let us not lose from sated eyes
The gift of wonder there—the glad surprise.

Let miracles be ours, awesome things—
The deepened sense of reverence wonder brings.
As stars of Heaven lose their distance far,
Let it not dim the glory of the star.

Let us not lose the vision and the dream
In bitter conquest, calculated scheme;
Nor cease to marvel at the Unseen Hand
That guides the fortunes of this Wonderland.

Give us a humbleness within the heart
To see that God and man each plays a part,
That we may heed the call of frontier skies,
The light of reverent wonder in our eyes.

Glory Forever

What a grand old world we live in,
  Spite of all its wars and strife—
What a glorious adventure
  To the heart in love with life!

There's a glory in the sunrise
  Of each fresh new day begun,
A satisfying glory in
  A good day's work well done.

The glory of enchantment
  At the beautiful and fair,
A glorious awareness
  Of God's Presence everywhere.

A gladness and a glory
  In each friendship, old and new,
A glowing loyalty and trust
  That keeps those friendships true.

A sweet and wondrous glory
  In the love of man and maid;
A deep and gentle glory—
  Facing newness unafraid.

A thrilling, tingling glory
  In the mysteries of earth;
An awesome, reverent glory
  In the miracle of birth.

A radiance and glory
  In each challenge met and won;
A dignity and glory
  When the race of life is run.

A splendid, shining glory
  Like an aura that surrounds
The world of him within whose heart
  The love of life abounds.

Stand Tall

Stand tall—reach high!
You personify
The image of God above!
Be glad you are you,
Lay claim to your due
Of glorious life and love!

Shifting Sands

Are the sands of your young son's values
    Shifting before your eyes—
Assuming new shapes and proportions,
    Weird levels, strange patterns, odd size?
Be glad. It's a sign that he's growing.
    His mind is casting away
The outgrown cloak of the callow youth
    He was—but yesterday.
It's a sign that, at least, he is groping
    Toward whatever truth he can see—
A sign that he's growing in stature,
    Approaching maturity.

If you see the sands of his values
    Ashift in this changing world,
Don't panic in fear as you watch them
    Twisted and blown and swirled.
Down underneath all the shifting—
    Solid and firm and true—
Are the real basic truths you have taught him;
    In time they will all show through.
Be patient and understanding;
    The loose sand will soon blow away,
And a man will stand upon solid ground
    Where those sands are shifting today.

Somehow I Know

I have never seen the whole sea—
    And yet I know the sea,
For I've felt its cooling waters
    And I've heard it speak to me.

I can't conceive a total God,
    And yet I know Him well,
For I've felt His quiet Presence
    In a way words cannot tell.

I've never seen the air around,
    And yet I breathe the air.
I cannot see the God I love,
    But oh, I know He's there!

Walk in the Woods

Walk carefully, walk prayerfully,
Let no harsh sound debase
The deep cathedral quiet
Of this holy wooded place;
Let no discordant thought or word
Disturb the peace that fills
The sacred sanctuary
Of this temple in the hills.

Today is Enough

Why are we here? This thing we call our soul—
Has it a Yesterday? A future goal?
Why was it sent to roam this teeming earth
By way of that great miracle called birth?

But does it matter so? Why must we borrow
Concern from Heaven's Past and God's Tomorrow?
Today is all that counts—a little light
Between those two dark secrets of the night.

Today is all we have and all we know—
And He who sent us meant it to be so.
The human mind, so finite small of span,
Could not envisage all of God's great plan.

Why are we here? What matters why? We are.
Perhaps our soul has traveled long and far
To reach this island haven in the sky;
Perhaps it soon will bid this earth goodbye.

But Yesterday and all Infinity
God mercifully screens from you and me.
It is enough to live and love Today
And trust in Him to show our souls the way.

The Challenge of Our Doubts

We ought not be alarmed if doubts
  Torment us now and then;
Doubts are the pruning shears that give
  Our faith new strength again.
Doubts are the gusty winds that bend
  Our old beliefs to earth.
Those that spring back firm, we know
  Are rooted deep in worth.

Faith must have its element
  Of doubt. If all were known
Of life and life hereafter, knowledge
  Would suffice alone—
But faith—belief—is based upon
  The things we cannot see.
Without the challenge of our doubts
  Believing could not be.

The questing mind of man will ever
  Seek the "how" and "why,"
But faith is our response to that
  Beyond the seeing eye.
Our faith in unseen things gives life
  A meaning here below,
And doubts are summer showers
  That help that faith to grow.

I Cannot Teach You

I cannot teach you, though the years
    Have led me farther on
Along the path of life than you
    In your short span have gone.

I can but lead you to the threshold
    Of your thinking mind,
And leave you there to search the worth
    Of such as you may find.

I can but point the way, then you
    Must trudge your road alone;
The crossroads you will meet will not be
    Those that I have known.

I cannot teach you, I can only
    Take you by the hand
And lead you to the point where you
    Can see the Promised Land.

The rest of it is up to you,
    The choice is yours to make—
And I can only pray that 'tis
    The right road you will take.

To Save a Rose

If we can, in our living day by day,
Save but one rose of all that grace our way—
One rose preserved through frost of strife and sorrow
To bloom again tomorrow—and tomorrow.

If we can save one sunset's lingering gold,
Of all the many sunsets life will hold—
One sunset saved to shed its peace on earth
When shades of hate and war obscure life's worth.

If we can save just one ennobling thought
Of all the knowledge man has ever sought—
One thought to spark the light of truth again,
Then you and I will not have lived in vain.

A Cushioning of Prayer

Prayer fits into any little corner of the day
Like packing round this treasure we call life,
Cushioning the bruises and the knocks along the way,
Lessening the crush of cares and strife.
So pack your day with bits of prayer lest damages of sin
And doubt and fear leave ugly markings there;
Keep it firm and steady—that treasured life within,
Protect it with a cushioning of prayer.

Fallen Idol

So your idol of gold—that wondrous one
  You worshiped with awe from afar,
Has proven to be but a little tin god
  No better than most humans are.

And you're disillusioned and crushed and hurt,
  Resentful of Fate's low blow,
That he, who inspired such faith and trust,
  Should abuse your trusting so.

But think—did you worship him for himself,
  Or could it have possibly been
The fire he kindled within your own heart
  That made seeming gold of his tin?

Could it have been that you fashioned of him
  The image of all you admired,
And vested in him all the fine golden traits
  That he, in that image, inspired?

If your golden idol has turned to tin,
  Be not wholly unconsoled—
A coating of tin can reflect the sun's rays
  As brightly as one of pure gold.

Be glad for the light he has shed your way,
  The joy he has brought to you.
What matter the tin or the feet of clay?—
  The dreams he inspired are true.

The visions you saw as you looked on him
  Were worthy and genuine.
God's instruments are not always gold—
  Sometimes He molds them of tin.

Hold Fast a Dream

Hold fast a dream. On this careening earth
It takes a firm, bright dream to give life worth,
The dignity, the meaning we desire,
The glowing purpose there, the burning fire.
One splendid, all-consuming dream held high
Against the dark and cloud-bewildered sky—
One steady, changeless, dream-inspired goal
Makes all of life a challenge to the soul,
A glorious challenge nothing else can give—
Hold fast a dream if you would truly live!

King's-X

Remember how we used to call
  "King's-X" in games we played
Whenever we were winded
  Or repairs had to be made—
And how the magic of that call
  Would stop the game's mad pace
Until we'd caught our breath again
  To go on with the race?

Sometimes I think we might do well
  To call "King's-X" on life
And take a little time out
  From its worry and its strife—
A moment's breather now and then
  To catch up with our thinking,
Till we can face life's trials again
  Courageous and unshrinking.

Best for Me

How often I've been put to test
To make the best of second-best,
Only to wake one day and see
The second-best was best for me.

The Heart Knows

The French have a saying,
   And surely it is so—
"The heart knows reasons
   Reason doesn't know."
The heart knows reasons
   Reason cannot find
Within the coldly calculating
   Chambers of the mind.

The heart has ways of knowing,
   Strange, angel-whispered ways,
We can't explain in logic
   Or express in simple phrase,
But deep within we know it points
   The way that we should go—
The heart has its own reasons,
   Reason cannot know.

Something to Live For

Something to live for—this the need
  Of every living soul,
A deep, inherent yearning for
  A purpose and a goal;
A something bigger than ourselves
  To put us to the test,
A high and splendid something
  That demands our very best.

Someone to care for—this another
  Need implanted there.
We have an inborn need to love,
  To cherish and to share;
Someone whose every wish we hold
  Above our own desires—
A someone who our highest dreams
  And finest self inspires.

Since time began, the heart of man,
  No matter what the cost,
Must have a goal—must have a love—
  Without them all is lost.
These are the basic needs of life,
  God-given from above—
Something that we can live for—
  Someone that we can love.

The Sound of Laughter

God must receive so many solemn prayers,
I think that He must relish now and then
A chuckle one in joy of living shares—
The sound of laughter from His world of men.

For faith—real, honest faith's a joyous thing,
Not easily compressed in hardbound rules,
And Heaven's not where angels fear to sing,
Nor laughter meant to be confined to fools.

And if, in midst of prayer's solemnities,
An errant thought strays off to meet a smile,
I think that God smiles, too, at what He sees—
And both are made the happier for the while.

I Will Not Fail

It may not make it across the sea,
This frail craft bearing the soul of me;
The winds are rough and the waves are high,
And the sea has defeated stronger than I.
But I cannot wait for the winds to still,
So I set my sails and heave to with a will—
And I battle the waves, and the waves fight back,
The night is dark and the skies are black,
And I may go down in the roiling tide—
But I will not fail—for I will have tried.

A Word of Praise

I spoke a word of praise today,
One I had no real need to say—
I spoke a word of praise to one
Commending some small service done,
And in return, to my surprise,
I reaped rewards of mountain size;
For such a look of pleasure shone
Upon his face—I'll never own
A gift more beautiful to see
Than that swift smile he gave to me.
I spoke one little word of praise
And sunshine fell on both our ways.

Home Again

The house was fast asleep when we returned.
It creaked and groaned a little as we stood
Within the open door and fed our eyes
On old familiar things. Oh, it was good
To be back home again from foreign land!
We'd slept in castles hundreds of years old,
We'd visited cathedrals tall and grand,
But all of that was tinsel—this was gold.
So still it was, we almost tiptoed in.
John moved to start the old grandfather clock.
We'd really never realized how much
We'd missed the comfort of its soft tick-tock.
We felt the old place stir to wakefulness
As shades were opened on its sleepy eyes.
Its smile grew wider with each ray of sun,
And you could almost hear its glad surprise—
"You're home again! Oh, welcome, welcome home!"
Perhaps it was for this we had to go—
Our eyes could only see from far away.
It took those miles between to help us know
The precious dearness of our everyday.

Be Friends with Yourself

Stand back and take a good look
   At this person that you are.
In some respects he may be
   Just a little under par,
But then I'm sure you'll find
   That he has many virtues, too.
You ought to get acquainted
   And be better friends, you two.

For faults are often curable
   With just a little care.
Bring them out into the open
   And you're more than halfway there.
It could even be those faults are
   Really talents in disguise,
Waiting there to be discovered
   By your more reflective eyes.

Since you have to live together
   All your life—yourself and you—
It's important that yourself approves
   Of what you say and do;
It's important that you treat yourself
   With honor and respect,
For the world will base its measure
   On what you, yourself, expect.

Stand back in introspection,
  Be as honest as you can
In your secret self-appraisal
  Of your own soul's inner man.
You may find you rather like him—
  You'll be happier in the end
And you'll be a better person
  If you let him be your friend.

Unless a Love be Free

Love cannot be held in bonds.
  Unless a love be free,
And freely given from the heart,
  That love will cease to be.

The bonds of love cannot be tied;
  There is no power on earth
That can restrain a heart's true love
  Or bound its depth and girth.

For love—of all of Heaven's gifts—
  Must ride on angel wing—
It cannot be constrained with bonds,
  A fettered, grounded thing.

Pick Yourself a Star

So you've a dream—well, so have I—
It's something we all do,
And yet the dreams that really reach
The stars are mighty few.
For most of us are cowards—
We're frightened of the night,
Afraid to trust our dreams beyond
The limits of our sight.

We anchor them with lack of faith,
We hold them down with ropes
Of doubt and fear and hopelessness—
Or we depend on hopes
And wistful wishing only
To make our dream come true,
And fail to realize our hands
Must help a little, too.

It takes hard work and courage,
Vision—faith—these are the wings
That give a dream the strength to soar
No matter what life brings.
These are the wings that carry
Our day-dreams high and far—
So give your dream a pair of wings
And pick yourself a star!

I'm Glad

I'm glad the great Creator
   Arranged for there to be
A bit of work left over
   For the likes of you and me.

I'm sure He could have finished things—
   For instance—made the bread,
But no—He chose to give us little
   Grains of wheat, instead.

I'm sure He could have planted houses
   With no strain nor fuss;
Instead, He planted trees and left
   The building up to us.

I think He wanted us to share
   That joy and sheer elation
That builders and creators know
   Who see their own creation.

Station LOVE

I believe love travels on the air
As surely as our voices carry there.
I believe the heart attuned can feel
The closeness of its presence, warm and real.

I believe that we can send our love
On silent waves of ether high above,
And that, somehow, that love will find its way
To reach and brighten up our loved one's day.

I believe the love that we impart
Has wave-lengths stretching outward from the heart
Of power never dreamed of, matchless worth,
To make a better, more harmonious earth.

I believe if we could only know
How wide and far this love of ours can go,
How powerful its strength to lift and leaven—
We'd use that love to make this world a Heaven.

Love Speaks

Love speaks in such a silent voice
  Without a word,
And yet there never was a voice
  More clearly heard.

Love moves among us softly as
  A wraith unseen,
And yet a thing more real and true
  Has never been.

Love works its wonders quietly
  Without a sound,
And yet we see its evidence
  In all around.

Love speaks in whispers—yet its
  Mighty will
Can move a mountain—make the world
  Stand still.

We Ought to Have a Glory

We ought to have a glory
  In our living every day.
We ought to spread a glory
  Round about us all the way.

For, surely, if the story
  That the Good Book tells is true,
The glory of God's image should
  Shine out in me and you.

The joy of our believing
  Should shine out for all to see
In a glory radiating
  From plain folks like you and me.

Yes, we ought to have a glory
  That folks can see and feel—
A sort of living story
  Of a faith that's true and real.

Make Way!

Remove the barriers, clear the road,
  Great dreams are on the way!
Prepare the highway to bear the load,
  Great dreams are due today!

Dreams that were but fantasy
  A yesterday ago—
Dreams to be reality
  Far sooner than we know.

They're only passing through Today—
  This world of you and me;
They're heading toward Tomorrow-land,
  That magic world to be!

But we can line the way and cheer,
  Spectators, you and I—
Hats off! Make way! And a big Hooray!
  Great dreams are passing by!

Thank You

Must I say only "Thank you"?
Upon these two small words
Must I entrust my gratefulness to you?
So often lightly spoken
As often lightly heard,
It seems too great a task for them to do.

But I have warmed and fed them
From the depths of my heart's store,
And send them on their journey strong and well,
And pray that when you hear them
You will open your heart's door
And listen to the story they would tell.

Ah, now your answering message comes,
And oh, it brings to me
All life can ever need to make it good.
I hear the words, "You're welcome"—
Your tender smile I see,
And know my "Thank you" has been understood.

Who Do You Work For?

"Who do I work for?—Myself," he said,
With a smile and a toss of his proud young head.
"I work for myself and my family—
I've a wife, you know, and a baby-to-be;
And I work for my neighbors. I guess every man
Needs a hand sometimes, and I help where I can.
Oh yes, I work for the good Lord, too;
There are quite a few things He needs my hands to do.
Of course (and he named the Company)
I depend on them for my salary.
I work for them, too, and I earn my pay,
Eight good hours of work a day.
Excuse me, sir, if I seem to mock—
I have to go now and punch the clock—
If I sounded facetious, excuse it please,
But I really do work for all of these."

To Irene

The glow of friendliness shone in her face;
She greeted great and small with equal grace;
She radiated warmth and love and light—
Somehow, her smile made all the world seem right.

She left a legacy of priceless worth
To all whose lives her life had touched on earth—
A memory that time cannot erase—
That glow of friendliness upon her face.

Inspiration in Despair

There is an inspiration
To be found in deep despair.
The heart in desperation
Will seek relief through prayer.
When all the human aids have failed
And life is darkest night,
The eyes of man, instinctively,
Will turn toward the Light.
The soul of man cries out for help
And finds that God is there—
There is an inspiration
To be found in deep despair.

May His Hand be on Your Shoulder

May His hand be on your shoulder
Through these trying hours and days,
His Guiding Light surround you
As you tread these shadowed ways.
May you know His warmth as sadness
Breaks its cold wave on your shore;
May you feel His love enfold you
With a faith sound and secure.
May His Presence close beside you
Give you strength to carry on,
Trusting in His tender promise
Of a new and brighter dawn.

I Wish You Happiness

I wish you happiness—God's gift
To cleanse and heal and warm and lift.
Despite the warring times, the grief,
Perplexity and disbelief,
Hope still revives with each new sun—
And hope and happiness are one;
Faith still refuses to give ground,
And faith with happiness is bound.
I could not wish you more—nor less—
Than Heaven's gift of happiness.

The People Grower

He has a sort of green thumb
   When it comes to handling folks.
He'll listen to their troubles,
   He'll chuckle at their jokes.
Somehow they know his interest
   Is genuine and true,
And right before your eyes you'll see
   Them grow an inch or two.
You'll see their faces blossom out
   In smiles of budding cheer.
You know they've found a ray of hope
   To drive away their fear;
You know he's sowed the seeds of faith
   And showered them with love,
And made them sense the presence
   Of the good Lord up above.
He clears out all the weeds of doubt
   And fear and hate and greed
And gives them room to breathe. He seems
   To sense their every need.

He nurtures them with praises for
  The good things that they've done
And trains them to look upward
  And to stand tall in the sun.
He has a sort of green thumb
  Like a farmer with the sod—
But his work is growing people
  In the image of his God.

The Reason Why

I've a halo to live up to,
One quite undeserved, that's true,
But if someone placed a halo
On your head—what would *you* do?

Would you brush aside the brightness
Of their trust and deep belief?
Would you laugh away the halo
And bring that love to grief?

I've a halo to live up to,
Though I know I can but try;
But if I'm standing taller now
You'll know the reason why.

Power to Lift

If God has given you the special power
Of lightening another's shadowed hour;
If others turn to you for help in need,
Then is your life a blessed one, indeed.

But if, by Grace Divine, yours is the gift
To cheer men's lives—to comfort and to lift,
By that same token yours the power, too,
To wound those others who look up to you.

However great our power to upraise
And change another's life by word of praise,
Just so great is our power to crush and bruise,
If we that special gift of God abuse.

So if the God of Love has chosen you
To trust His labors of compassion to,
Oh, take care lest you use His precious gift
To hurt those who look up to you to lift.

Possessed of a Dream

A dream isn't really something you have
   So much as that it "has" you.
The greater the dream, the stronger its hold
   On all you say and do.

Persistent, possessive, it demands
   With dominating power,
Your best in every word and deed
   Of every waking hour.

It lends an urgency to life,
   A challenge and a dare,
And though the road you trudge be rough,
   Your spirit walks on air!

A dream is not a thing possessed—
   The dream possesses you;
And only in that dream fulfilled
   Do you, yourself, come true.

Ragamuffin Day

Today was a ragamuffin day—
A devil-may-care, let-come-what-may,
Happy-go-lucky—you know the kind—
A day that paid Duty not one whit of mind.

Ragged and tattered, with chores half done,
It blithely ignored them to romp in the sun.
It danced and made faces at those who would be
The solemn exponents of sobriety.

A mischievous wastrel that wouldn't face facts,
A raggedy clown—a laugh between acts,
It sang for no reason save singing alone—
Yet it was as fruitful a day as I've known,

For it left me a smile, and it gave me to see
The thing of sheer joy that life sometimes can be.
I gave it a wink as I waved it goodbye,
And I swear it winked back at me there from the sky.

In Case a Tree Grows There

We used to have a peach tree;
No one planted it at all,
And how it chanced to grow there
No one ever could recall.
Some careless hand had dropped a seed—
Whose hand we'll never know—
And time and circumstance conspired
To cause that seed to grow.
And every year that peach tree
Grew the finest fruit around.
No sweeter, plumper peaches
In the whole town could be found.

It's like that sometimes with a word;
We drop it carelessly
And it takes root in someone's life
And grows to be a tree.
Sometimes the fruit it bears
Would make us proud if we could know
That it was some stray word of ours
That caused that tree to grow.
It rather seems as though we ought
To use a little care
About the kind of words we drop,
In case a tree grows there.

Corner Cupboard

When I was just a little girl,
A long-gone yesterday,
We had a corner cupboard
Where Mother cached away
The most intriguing odds and ends
A child could wish to see.
A veritable treasure house
That cupboard was to me!

She kept her favorite trinkets there,
And I will never know
A more enchanting picture.
She, too, must have loved them so.
I still can see each trinket
Placed with such care on its shelf.
I know now that those trinkets
Formed a portrait of herself.

I'm sure my mother never dreamed
That in the days to be
I'd pick her corner cupboard
To hold in memory.
We never know what children
Will be storing as they play,
To color their remembering
Of this—their Yesterday.

As I recall that cupboard
And how dear its memory yet,
I wonder what my child's world holds
Her heart will not forget.
I wonder what she's finding,
All unbeknownst to me,
In my life's corner cupboard
To enrich her memory.

To One No Longer Here

I never think of her without a smile—
And that's a rather splendid thing to say.
What better legacy could one bequeath
Than smiles to brighten up a loved one's day?

I miss her, but I find when teardrops start
And when I'm feeling lonely and bereft,
Just thinking of her starts me smiling, too,
At all the happy memories she left.

Back Home

Strange, isn't it—of all the places
  We may live and roam,
Somehow, we always single out
  One place we call "Back home."

We never know exactly why
  We set this place apart,
And keep it so enshrined within
  The memory of our heart.

But always in our thinking,
  For no reason we can give,
We use the phrase "Back home" for that
  One place we used to live.

Is it, perhaps, because it was
  The scene of happy days
And left such pleasant memories
  We treasure them always?

Could it be we became aware
  Of life's full meaning there,
And that is why we take its memory
  With us everywhere?

Or were our roots so deeply bedded
    In its warm, rich loam,
We never can quite lose our sense
    Of oneness with that home?

Whatever be the reason for
    Our strange nostalgic choice,
When someone says, "Back Home," we know
    We hear the heart's own voice.

Left-Over Laughter

I love you most, I think
For all the smiles left in your wake,
The way my heart keeps chuckling
At the memories you make.

I love you for the glorious fun
We have when we're together,
The way you always bring the sun,
No matter what the weather—

But most of all I love you
For the joy that lingers after
And fills the times between with bits
Of bright left-over laughter.

Wagonful of Walnuts

Along about this time of year,
  September through November,
We kids would get our wagons out—
  Oh, surely you remember—
And trek out to the woods nearby,
  A mile or maybe two,
Down by the creek (we called it crick)
  Where the big black walnuts grew.

Each nut was covered over
  With a hard, round greenish ball,
And we'd pile them in our wagons—
  We could never take them all—
And then we'd trudge back home
  And spread them in the sun to dry
Up atop the old shed roof—
  That's when the days crept by!
But finally the time would come
  To haul our treasures down,
The hard green balls reduced now
  To a crusty shell of brown.

With a hammer and an old flatiron
   We'd knock the covering loose.
The hands of every kid in town
   Were stained with walnut juice.
But oh, the joy of munching on
   Those morsels rich and sweet.
In all the years I've never known
   A more delicious treat.

Along about this time each year
   I'd give a lot to pick
A wagonful of walnuts
   From those trees down by the crick.

Where Once Her Lilacs Grew

Spring slipped in through the garden gate
And looked about to learn
How many of the flowers
Had awaited her return.
I think she must have been surprised
And rather saddened, too,
To see an ugly high board fence
Where once her lilacs grew.

First Frost

Isn't it odd the memories
We cling to from the past?
Such simple sights and sounds and smells,
And yet they last and last.
   You take an autumn day like this
   When frost is in the air—
   The hush of doomsday all about,
   You feel it everywhere.
On days like this I leave behind
My city home and go
In memory back to those autumn
Days I used to know.
   I see the big old kitchen,
   Steamy-warm with smells so good!
   And Mother baking pumpkin pies
   As only Mother could.
I see my Father coming,
See the old brown scarf he wore,
And feel the rush of cold, fresh air
As he comes in the door.
   I see him warm his hands
   Above the range and hear him say,
  "We'll catch it sure tonight.
   Old Winter's really on its way."

And Mother answers, "Maybe not,
But we'll not take a chance.
I'd better hustle out and bring in
Those tomato plants."
    Then from the warm old wraps that
    Always hung close by the door
    We bundle up in readiness
    To do this last fall chore.
And out into the twilight gray,
The air so brittle clear
Our very voices leave a hollow
Echo on the ear.
    On to the patch of garden where
    The prize tomatoes grow,
    To save their precious harvest
    From the wintry winds that blow.
We pick the ripe and half-ripe ones
(They'll ripen on the sill)
Then pull the crisp, green, spicy plants
(Seems I can smell them still!)
    We carry them up to the house
    And down the cellar stair
    And hang them upside down to ripen
    In the darkness there.
There never is a frosty day—
September through November—
That doesn't whisper to my heart,
"Remember—oh, remember?"

The Old Church Bell

I remember so well the old church bell
  In the town where I was born,
How its cheery sound would call the town
  To worship Sunday morn.

"It's a beautiful day," it seemed to say,
  "Of all the week the best.
It won't be long till the opening song,
  So hurry up now—get dressed!"

At Christmas time, how its mellow chime
  Would echo across the snow.
I wish I could tell the thrill of that bell
  Those Christmas Eves long ago.

When someone died, how the whole town cried
  At the tolling of the bell,
Yet we always found it a comforting sound,
  A solemn and fitting farewell.

And how it rang out with laugh and a shout
  When a wedding was under way!
"Come along!" it cried, "Josh the groom, kiss the bride!
  It's a glorious wedding day!"

I shall never forget—I can hear it yet
　　With all of its magic power—
The town's ringing voice—to weep or rejoice—
　　The bell in the old church tower.

Bless This Little Chapel

Bless this little chapel, Lord,
　　Let all who enter feel
Within the quiet of these walls
　　Thy Presence close and real.

Make of it a shrine of love,
　　A friendly, warm retreat,
Where weary souls may rest awhile
　　From turmoil of the street.

Lay Thy benediction
　　On each service that it sees,
That it may be a hallowed place
　　Of sacred memories.

Bless this little chapel,
　　And may it ever be
A place where reaching hearts may find
　　A closer bond with Thee.

Small-Town, U.S.A.

Have you paid a visit recently
  To Small-Town, U.S.A.?
If not, I highly recommend you do.
You will find a different outlook
In their simple, honest way—
A fresh perspective, interesting and new.

There's a quiet friendly atmosphere
  That permeates the air—
You feel it more the longer that you stay;
A warm, refreshing feeling
That your neighbors really care
And welcome you to Small-Town, U.S.A.

There's a gentle, earthy feeling there—
  A sort of "peace-on-earth"
That wraps around your heart and makes you see
That life can be more meaningful,
A thing of much more worth
Than what you might have figured it to be.

Yes, if you haven't been there,
   I suggest you take a day,
A week, a month—whatever you can spare,
And pay a little visit
To Small-Town, U.S.A.—
It's just around the bend from Anywhere.

The Important Thing

It's nice to be important,
To stand out above the crowd;
It's nice to feel you've earned the right
To hold your head up proud.
It's nice to feel important,
To be sought out for advice—
But important people know
It's more important to be nice.

The Long-Haired Male of the Species

I believe in evolution,
  Although I must admit
I've a very hazy notion
  What exactly's meant by it.

The explosion of the nucleus-
  Primeval leaves me cold,
And, really now, who cares about
  Things millions of years old.

Primordial clouds of gases,
  All whirling round in space—
Condensations, galaxies,
  My small mind can't embrace.

A solar system, gravitation,
  Planets, protoplasms—
And man evolving finally
  Through ectoplasmic spasms.

Those "brains" who tell us how it was—
  I'd never underrate 'em.
I can't conceive, but I believe
  Their weird tales, all verbatim.

But when the Guiding Powers see
   The end result that's shown—
I wonder if they might wish they'd
   Let well enough alone.

When I look on this newest creature
   Of the whole creation—
This howling, hairy idol
   Of our young world's adulation,

I think of all the zillion years
   It took to finally birth it,
And can't help wondering sometimes
   If it was really worth it.

Let's Go!

Why is it that a steering wheel
   Will cause a man to be
A changed, and absolutely different
   Personality?

You take a man I know—in fact,
   I know him very well;
I've cooked his meals and darned his sox
   More times than I could tell.

And normally he's very nice,
   Quite affable and sweet,
But what a change of face when he
   Gets in the driver's seat!

He really "drives defensively"
   For when he starts to drive,
He's sure the whole world's out to get him
   Come dead or alive!

The other drivers all are in cahoots
   To wreck his day;
They're idiots who have no business
   Driving, anyway.

He talks to each and every one
    Although they never know;
And every red light in the town
    Has heard his bark, "Let's Go!"

The other fellow takes his lane
    Quite purely out of spite,
Another beats him to the only
    Parking place in sight.

When, finally, we get back home
    And up our own driveway,
He heaves a sigh of great relief—
    He's had a long, hard day.

It's quite amazing, really—
    He gets out and stretches—then
He grins his normal grin and he's
    My own sweet guy again.

Thank Heaven for the Weather

Thank Heaven for the weather—
That old conversation piece.
How it saves an awkward moment;
How its every small caprice
Provides a welcome subject,
A common meeting place
Where the garrulous and tongue-tied
Can join in with equal grace.

Thank Heaven for the weather—
Rain or snow or fair or foul—
It's a subject all can handle
With the wisdom of an owl.
It's a happy silence breaker,
In good taste, no matter what;
And the nicest thing about it—
It's a thing we've always got!

Waste Not, Want Not

"Waste not, want not"—the quaint old phrase
    Was Grandma's stock in trade.
Her children cleaned their well-stocked plates
    Before one of them played.

"Waste not, want not"—I tried to make
    The phrase my motto, too,
But somehow, it won't work for me
    The way it used to do.

I clean my plate and then I eat
    The scraps left unconsumed,
Then wonder, when I check my weight,
    Why it seems to have zoomed!

I'm penny-wise; my thrifty ways
    To Grandma can be traced.
I waste not—but believe me,
    I want not this growing waist!

It's Contagious

Cheer is a contagious thing—
  The tiniest of smiles
Is apt to spread it all around
  For miles and miles and miles.

A single friendly handclasp
  Has been known to evoke
A downright epidemic
  In a whole roomful of folk.

Why, just a nod in passing
  And a hearty, cheery "Hi!"
Will make a smile break out
  On even strangers passing by.

The spread of cheer through laughter
  Is a proven thing and sure.
Affected hearts grow lighter—
  And they've never found a cure.

Yes, cheer is most contagious,
  But there never yet has been
A fatality recorded—
  So go ahead and grin!

September Hills

Have you seen the hills in September—
The aspens dripping their gold?
It's a picture no artist has painted,
A beauty no poet has told.

You must see for yourself the splendor
The glory that fills and thrills—
The gold of the sun on the aspens,
September high in the hills.

To stand by the road in the silence,
And feel the Divine Presence there,
The touch of the Master Artist
So evident everywhere.

To sense how the summer in dying
Has rallied its finest parade
And exits with banners flying,
Triumphant and unafraid.

If you've not seen the hills in September,
You must—for you'll never behold
A lovelier sight to remember
Than aspens' shimmering gold.

Greater the Soul

I looked upon a mountain high,
In grandeur rising to the sky,
And then I contemplated me—
How very small I seemed to be.

Yet in this fragile frame of mine
God chose to house a soul divine—
Not in that glorious, sun-crowned peak,
But in this body, frail and weak.

God chose to give to you and me
The promise of Eternity—
A child of His—can such be small?
A soul is surely Heaven-tall.

The mountain stands that I might see
How greater is the soul of me.

Comes Twilight Now

Comes twilight now—of all the day the best.
The huddled hills draw closer to earth's breast;
A hush of deep awareness fills the air,
The peace of vesper-time is everywhere.

The sense of Heaven's nearness gentles all—
The mighty mountain peaks, the wild bird's call;
The turmoil of the busy day subdued
As twilight lends its soft beatitude.

The heart recounts its treasures, one by one.
The glowing embers of the dying sun
Crown each with glory now, as twilight brings
Its rosary of joy in simple things.

Enchanted Land

Keep a little wonder
In your heart if you would live
To know the full enchantment
Life on earth was meant to give.

A little sense of marvel
As you go your daily way,
Amazement at the miracles
That crowd our every day.

A glad anticipation
Of happy happenings,
A buoyant faith in all things good
No matter what life brings.

A silent awe and reverence
Before that mystic Power
Revealed in majesty of stars
And in the smallest flower.

Keep a sense of wonder,
And your journey toward the truth
Will lead through that Enchanted Land
Of Everlasting Youth!